Amazon FBA For Beginners

A Step-by Step Guide To Starting and Launching a Successful Passive Income, E-Commerce Business

Robert E. Shore

Disclaimer

This book has been written for information purposes only. Every effort has been made to make this book as complete and accurate as possible. However, there may be mistakes in typography or content. Also, this book provides information only up to the publishing date. Therefore, this book should be used as a guide - not as the ultimate source.

The purpose of this book is to educate. The author and the publisher do not warrant that the information contained in this book is fully complete and shall not be responsible for any errors or omissions. The author and publisher shall have neither liability nor responsibility to any person or entity with respect to any loss or damage caused or alleged to be caused directly or indirectly by this book.

About the Author

Robert Shore is an entrepreneur living in the UK who loves sharing knowledge and helping others on the topic of business and business psychology.

He is a passionate person who will go the extra mile and over-deliver.

Some words of wisdom:

"I believe that knowledge is power. Everyone should improve themselves and/or business, no matter what stage in life they're in. Whether it's to develop a better mindset or to increase profits. Moving forward is key."

© Copyright 2019 by Robert E. Shore – All rights reserved.

The content contained within this book may not be reproduced, duplicated or transmitted without direct written permission from the author or publisher.

Under no circumstances will any blame or legal responsibility be held against the publisher, or author, for any damages, reparation, or monetary loss due to the information contained within this book, either directly or indirectly.

Legal notice:

This book is copyright protected. This book is only for personal use. You cannot amend, distribute, sell, use, quote or paraphrase any part, or the content within this book, without the consent of the author or publisher.

Table of Contents

Chapter 1 - An Introduction to Amazon FBA 1

Chapter 2 - Getting Started 4
Creating Your Account 4
Creating Listings 6
Sending the Stock 7

Chapter 3 – How to Choose a Niche and a Product 9
The Niche 10
Choosing the Best Product Types 11

Chapter 4 – How To Source Products 14
How To Choose a Product To Sell 16
Some Considerations 18
Packaging 19
Creating Attractive Packaging 19
Keep it Minimal 20
Keep it Safe 21
Make it Desirable and Think About Branding 22
Barcode 22

Chapter 5 – Marketing and Selling 23
Use AdSense 24
Run a Blog 24
Creating Buzz 25
More Options 26

Chapter 6 – Photography and Product Descriptions 27
Description 27
Photography 29
The Tools 29

The Setting 29

The Composition 30

Chapter 7 – SEO for Amazon Products 32

Keywords and Keyphrases 33

Rating and Reviews for Amazon Products 35

Chapter 8 – Alternative Options 37

Creating Your Own Products 37

Selling Beyond Amazon 38

Step 1 - Do Your Research 39

Step 2 - Know Yourself 39

Step 3 - Find Your Ally 40

Step 4 - Use a Sales Representative 40

Chapter 9 – Scaling Your Business 41

Basic Growth 41

Branding 42

Other Fulfilment Companies 43

Chapter 10 – Conclusion and Blueprint for Success 44

Chapter 11 - Checklist 47

What is Amazon FBA 47

Choosing Products 47

The Process 48

Encourage More Sales 49

More Options 50

Chapter 12 - The Most Crucial Resources 51

Useful Reads 55

Introduction

Amazon FBA is a service provided by Amazon to sellers that can help them to build highly successful reseller businesses far more quickly and effectively than would otherwise be possible. Here, a company is letting Amazon take care of the heavy lifting when it comes to storage and logistics, meaning that all the brand has to do is choose the right products and market!

Of course, it's a little more complex than all that!

But at the end of the day, what this service means is that a small entrepreneur or business is able to start selling products through the largest online store in the world, without having to invest huge amounts of money in infrastructure, stock, and staff. Now *anyone* can make a killing selling the next hit product, and in this book, you're going to learn exactly how to get started.

Chapter 1 - An Introduction to Amazon FBA

Let's start from the beginning: what exactly is Amazon FBA?

Essentially, FBA here stands for "Fulfilment By Amazon." This does exactly what it says on the tin: it means that Amazon will handle your fulfilment.

With FBA, you'll be able to outsource all of the most complicated, costly, and error-prone aspects of your business, and instead just focus on choosing products and selling them.

That's because Amazon will handle both storage and delivery, meaning that you just need to get the products shipped directly from the supplier/wholesaler to Amazon's warehouses (called "fulfilment centers" which sounds like some kind of self-help cult hideout).

Your product will then be listed on Amazon, and will then be fulfilled *via* Amazon. That means in other words, that Amazon will list your product on its storefront, and every time someone puts in an order, it will send it out to the buyer. This way, you can potentially fulfil hundreds of thousands of orders without needing to see a single product!

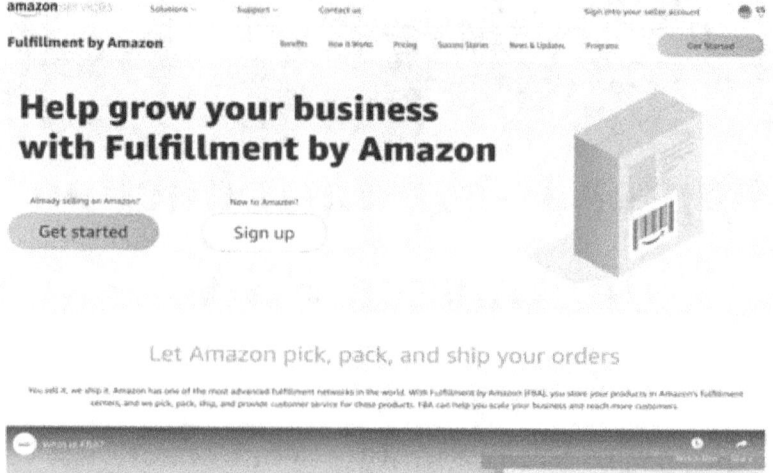

Of course you will pay fees, and there *are* particular regulations you need to abide by. But for the small business owner or entrepreneur, this is a FAR preferable scenario than having to have large amounts of inventory delivered to their home. And it opens up nearly endless opportunities. Your buyers can even benefit from Prime delivery and get their products *the very next day*.

Amazon Prime alone has over 95 million members in the US alone, and that's only 59% of the user base in that country! The site owns 49% of the eCommerce market in the US too.

By having your products listed on Amazon, they become *significantly* more likely to succeed –

especially as customers have become so used to buying on the platform with a single click.

And with Amazon handling the delivery, you'll have just a few fees to worry about and no logistics, tracking, or other stuff that can go wrong! Your customers will be getting a service that is comparable to the very biggest and best-known brands in the world.

As long as you choose the right products, invest wisely, and know how to write a great store listing… then you can't fail.

And you'll learn all of that over the next chapters of this book.

Chapter 2 - Getting Started

But before we go further, first you will need to understand how to start your business on Amazon.

You are going to need to sign up for an account so you can go ahead and start sourcing products. In this chapter, you'll learn how to set up your Amazon FBA account and you'll see your options.

You should create your account *before* you invest in any stock!

Creating Your Account

The first step is to go to: https://services.amazon.com
On the page, click Start Selling:

You'll then need to register your business details as shown below:

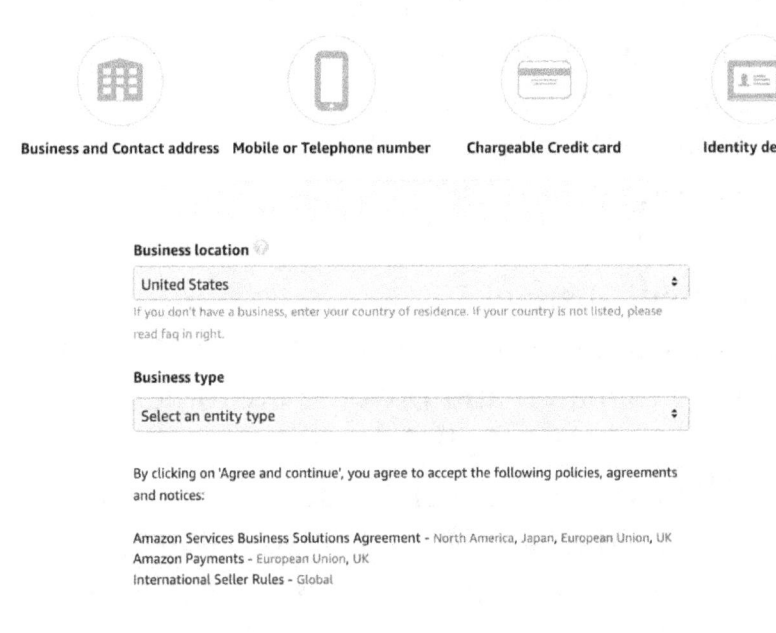

Follow the rest of the steps to complete your Seller account registration.

Creating Listings

In order to get started, you will need to start creating your listings. This is relatively easy fortunately! Just sign into the homepage and then find the inventory tab. Click "Add a Product" and then "Create a New Product Listing." You can then select the most relevant category for your product.

The next page may be a little overwhelming and is filled with fields to fill out. The good news is that a lot of these can be ignored, but things you will need to fill out include:

Item name (the name of your product as it will be seen by the customer)
Brand name (your business name)
Recommended Browse Node
Product ID (the IUPC number on the barcode)
Price
Fulfilment channel

For the last option you need to select "I want amazon to dispatch and provide customer service for my items if they sell."

You'll also need to write a description, add keywords, and more. We'll discuss how to choose the best options for all these things in future, but for now, all you need to do is to click save and finish!

Of course, you'll also need to set up a payment method, your business address, and all manner of additional details in order to sell effectively. But all of this is self-explanatory and should be easy to understand as you follow through the instructions.

Sending the Stock

Woah there! We haven't even chosen our products yet!

While this is true, it's useful to go through the set-up process now, just so that you know what you're going to be dealing with once you're ready to go.

If you chose Amazon as your fulfilment method, you will next be taken to a page titled "Send/Replenish Inventory."

Once you get to this point, you will need to provide more details for your item. That includes such things as the proportions of the item and the weight.

There are also some key requirements for all items that are going to be sent to Amazon. They all need to be labelled with a label that is unique to that item, with a shipment ID. This is an internal barcode Amazon will use in order to track and manage all of its inventory.

You can either get the freight forwarder to handle this for you, or you can pay Amazon to do it on your behalf. Using a freight forwarder is cheaper, but only slightly – and Amazon is easier to use!

Now you'll need to tell Amazon how the inventory will be delivered. You can pick "Small

Parcel Delivery" and "Amazon Partnered Carrier." This means that the factory will be able to send products to Amazon using a carrier that is approved by Amazon.

It's a good idea to make sure that all the boxes you send have a consistent size and weight, which will keep this easy to calculate. You'll need to *prepay* for the delivery based on the number and proportions of the boxes that you will sell. Amazon will generate a pre-paid label for you in the form of a PDF. You'll simply pass this on to the freight forwarder, and the freight forwarder will attach them to the cartons to give to the carrier to take over to Amazon!

The freight forwarder is of course the company that will take your products from the factory, through customs, and to the desired country. Seeing as many of the manufacturers you work with are going to be based in China, you will need a freight forwarder *as well* as a carrier at the other end (usually UPS) to bring your product to Amazon's warehouses.

After you've gone through all these steps, you'll be shown the cost of the shipment. Just click accept (assuming you do) and you can then proceed. That's everything done! All that is left is to wait for your parcels to arrive, at which point your listing will be live and people will be able to begin placing their orders. How exciting!

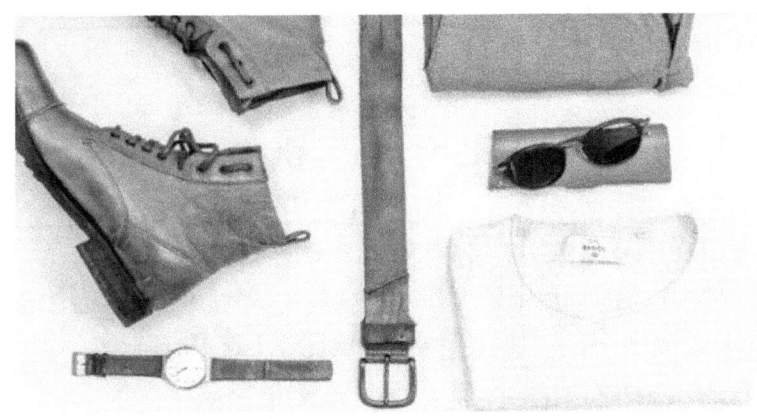

Chapter 3 – How to Choose a Niche and a Product

Okay, so now you understand the logistics of these logistics… you understand how to set up your Amazon account, you know the steps involved in the storage and the delivery, and you are ready to start sourcing and selling your products.

At this point, the next important step is to actually choose your products and decide what you want to sell. There are many factors to consider here, and it's very important that you take your time: the decision you ultimately make is going to dictate the trajectory and success (or otherwise) of your business going forward.

So how do you pick your niche and your product?

The Niche

I use the term "niche" because this is the internet marketing term you may be familiar with. In this case though, "industry" would be more appropriate. The product you sell is broadly going to fall into a category, whether that be fitness, health, money, fashion, grooming, pets, technology, or something else.

The industry you choose should be your first decision, as it will help you to narrow down the kinds of products you're going to sell and who you will sell to.

Keep in mind that you can likely find everything from extremely cheap items, to "big ticket" items, no matter what industry you choose. For instance, if you choose to sell tech products, then you could sell styluses and phone cases, or you could sell super-powerful computers! Don't let this be a factor that sways your decision then.

Common advice for authors is to "write what you know." This also applies here!

If you want to be successful, then choose a niche that you know inside out will help a huge amount. Not only does this allow you to choose products that you can appreciate yourself (meaning it's likely to appeal to other people like you), but you'll also be able to test it more thoroughly.

Moreover, if you're going to be content marketing and running social media accounts, then you're going to need to spend a lot of time reading and writing about the topic you've invested in. If you aren't at all interested in that subject matter, then this is going to come across and you'll find it *much* harder to become a thought leader.

Finally, if you *already* have a platform such as a blog, Facebook page, or YouTube channel, then of course you're going to want to leverage that by creating products you can sell to that same audience.

Other considerations such as demographic (who buys these products), whether the product category satisfies a need or a want, and how broadly appealing the niche is. The best advice for that latter question is to choose a category that balances the line between being too big and competitive and being too focussed and narrow.

Choosing the Best Product Types

Once you have your industry or product category, the next thing to consider is the actual specific product you want to sell. So if you're in fitness, are you going to sell dumbbells, resistance machines, protein shakes, or something else entirely.

Again, this comes down to many of the same factors as before:

Does the product make sense considering your own interests and any audience you've built?

Is the product broadly appealing within your niche, without being too over saturated?

Is this something that people really NEED or something they WANT? Is there an emotional drive behind that WANT?

Consider the value of a "consumable" product such as protein shake. These need to be replenished, and so if your buyers like what you offer, they can provide you with a steady, ongoing source of income!

We'll look at the individual pros and cons of specific items in terms of profits in the next chapter. But for now, some useful considerations to keep in mind are the value of the product.

A much more expensive product will require a bigger investment and will sell less frequently, but it will help you to make bigger profit in a shorter timeframe (assuming it sells). Larger items are also more expensive to ship (size and value don't always correlate). More expensive items are more difficult to replace as well.

Likewise, a less expensive product will let you invest in a much larger inventory, which in turn will mean you need to handle freight forwarding less often.

A good rule of thumb is to start with a less expensive product and work your way up. This will allow you to increase your total assets for reinvesting, and it will let you gain experience where the stakes are a little bit lower. Eventually, having a spread of different value products will make your business more resilient, and will mean you can appeal to all types of customers (it will also let you create a "funnel" of sorts).

Doing a bit of market research on Amazon is also always a good idea. A great tool is one called Jungle Scout (www.junglescout.com). This will let you do a deep search of Amazon to see the listings on Amazon and how much they are each selling per month. The service is a little expensive ($69) but you can always cancel it once you've done your research and chosen your products!

Again though, scratch your own itch! Think about what sells well, but also what you would actually use – and what you can really appreciate as being a useful thing to own.

Chapter 4 – How To Source Products

We've learned a lot by now, but still the entire thing is very abstract and hypothetical. That is to say that at this point, we don't actually have anything to sell!

So now we need to actually *find* the products we want to sell and get them shipped to Amazon. This does present a few challenges… but it's nothing we can't handle!

There are lots of places that you can find products to resell and of course you do have the option of going direct to the manufacturers. You can also opt to create your *own* products and get them shipped to Amazon!

But by far the most useful and efficient strategy for you, will be to use Alibaba (www.alibaba.com). Alibaba is to wholesalers what Amazon is to direct B2C sellers. That is to say that it provides an easy method to connect wholesalers to resellers; giving us a listing we can use to browse through the many different offerings on the site!

You can search for practically any product here, and you'll be presented with a selection of offerings from different warehouses, at different prices, with different minimum orders. You can then easily pick the one that best suits your needs, and then have it shipped direct to Amazon's fulfilment centers. The good news is that almost any company listing a product here will be more than happy to deliver to Amazon – it is functionally no different for them!

Many of these listings are "white label" products. This is exciting, because it means you can actually have your branding added to the product. The buyer will never know that a third party was involved, and that you didn't manufacture the product yourself!

How To Choose a Product To Sell

Now you know precisely the kind of thing you are looking for, you just need someone that is going to let you sell it on their behalf!

As mentioned, Alibaba sells just about every product under the sun, meaning that no matter what you want to sell, you will likely find a wholesaler to work with. If you can't find it, then you can always speak to one of the manufacturers about creating your own products! This is very standard practice and surprisingly easy to do.

But before you get carried away and choose your supplier, you first need to make sure that they meet all of Amazon's requirements, and that you will actually be able to make a profit for them.

First, look at the cost per unit of the item. That's how much *you* are going to pay for that product. Ask yourself if you can sell this at a high enough markup to make profit *after* the other associated costs.

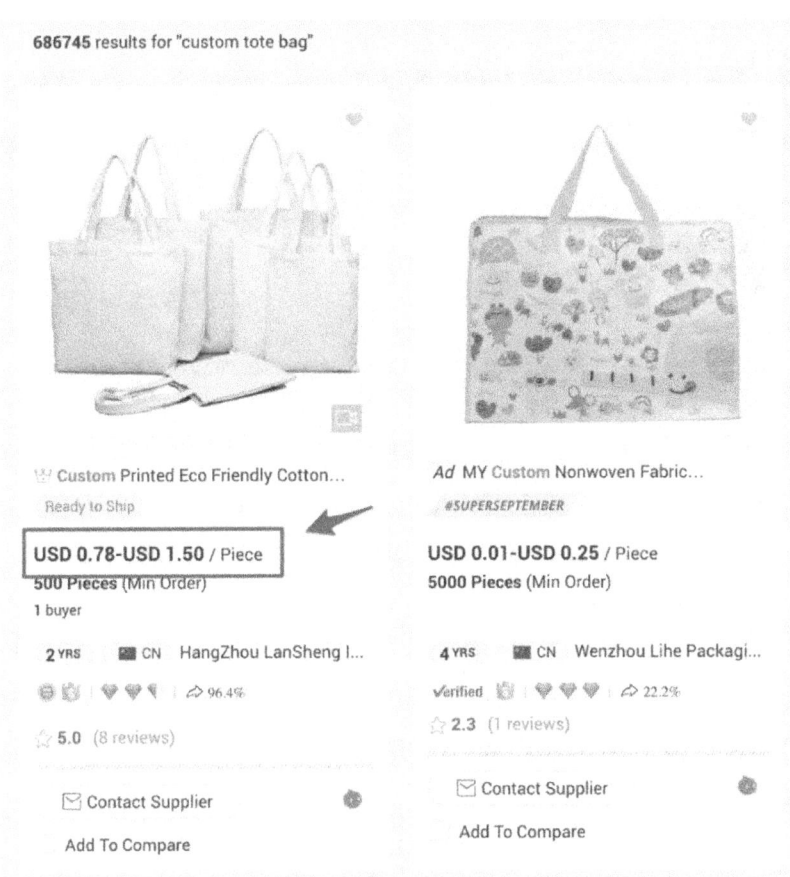

Remember, you're going to need to pay for:
The bulk order
Freight forwarding
Amazon's carrier
Amazon's fees
Potential returns
Any packaging
Any marketing

If you're giving yourself a headache trying to run this math, then you can use a tool like the AMZSCout FBA Free Calculator (https://amzscout.net/fba-fee-calculator/).

A general rule of thumb to remember, is that you will normally charge *twice* the cost per unit you pay. So if you buy jeans that cost $20 each per unit, then you will normally sell those on at $40 per unit. Just keep in mind what the competition is doing, whether your product is *worth* that much, and whether there is wiggle room for sales and discounts.

Keeping a spreadsheet also helps, and it's always a good idea to expect the worst.

Next, look at the minimum order. Some are very large (thousands) others are extremely small. In some cases, you can buy just two items, and then sell those through Amazon. If you're concerned about this whole notion and want to try a non-threatening sales strategy, then this is a brilliant way to go about it! Add two items to your listing, see if they sell, and know that you didn't lose that much money if they didn't!

Some Considerations

There are some things to keep in mind before you blow your wad on thousands of items.

First, you need to keep in mind FBA's policies. For example, Amazon does not permit any FBA prohibited substances to be sold on its site. Nor does it allow for hazardous materials. Certain categories will also require approval.

Find more policies here: https://sellercentral.amazon.com/

Next, you should consider the option of packaging…

Packaging

One of the most important factors to consider that many people forget meanwhile is packaging. It's absolutely crucial that you consider how you're going to package your items, not only to ensure that they arrive at their destination safely, but also to ensure that they are desirable for the customer and that they remain cost effective.

Amazon does not handle packaging for you, and if your items arrive loose then it won't forward them on. Some companies on Alibaba will agree to package for you, but it's very important that you ascertain this before ordering.

Moreover, while some companies might offer to add a poly bag, you should keep in mind that this won't always be enough to ensure your products arrive looking attractive. This is one of your few opportunities to increase brand awareness, so don't miss it!

Creating Attractive Packaging

If you want your products to come attractively packaged (rather than stuffed into a bag), then you will likely need to work with a packaging company and provide them with your files.

Before you begin, it's important to recognise that there are certain industry standards when it comes to packaging that you need to follow. For starters, your files should be saved in the .ai format if they are going to work with the vast majority of printers. That 'AI' stands for 'Adobe Illustrator' which is the tool that most companies will use to create their graphics - though there are cheaper alternatives.

It's also important to remember when designing your packaging that you need to include dielines. These lines act as placeholders, showing where you are going to need to diecut your graphics. Usually they will be saved as a separate layer in the file so that they can be removed before the final print, but it's important to use them as a guide when considering sizing, orientation etc. It's no good having a big image on the front of the box, but then having to fold or cut it straight down the middle.

Keep it Minimal

To get started, it's worth looking at some examples of other devices and their packaging. How is the Surface Pro packaged? The iPad? One thing you'll notice about all of these devices is that the packages are relatively small and minimalistic compared to what they used to be. This is something that makes sense both in terms of environmentalism, and in terms of profit margins. The less materials you use in creating your packaging, and the smaller you can keep it, the better it will be for the environment and the more money you will save on creating those items.

Minimalism is also currently very popular as a design trait - partly because of the pressures that have lead us to prefer saying more with less. Minimalism suggests class, and as it's also relatively cheap to produce, that's really the best of both worlds.

Keep it Safe

Of course the other important aspect of your packaging is that it needs to house the item inside safely and keep it secure. If you have a lose gadget rolling and sliding around inside a big empty box, then it will likely get damaged in transit, and that's something that you need to avoid. External packaging when sending will help with this, but you can improve your chances by including some bracing inside the box itself and potentially foam or other padding (most mobile phones have foam inside the box these days).

Amazon will provide additional packaging before it sends your packages to their destination, but this doesn't guarantee your item will get there in one piece. If you can add some additional padding in your own packaging, then you'll have more happy customers!

Make it Desirable and Think About Branding

Finally, you need to think of your packaging in terms of branding and marketing. One of the most important jobs of your packaging is to make your item look desirable so that people walking past it in stores will turn their heads. When someone is on the fence about making a purchase a great box can make all the difference. And in case they *don't* make a purchase, ensure your branding is prominent so that they can find the item again after they've mulled it over.

Barcode

In order to sell *any* product on Amazon with its own listing, you need to invest in a barcode. This is true whether you are creating new items, or whether you are reselling items from Alibaba.

Either way, a barcode is fortunately relatively easy to come across. You'll just need to order one from a site like SnapUPC (https://www.snapupc.com/buy-barcodes/).

This barcode will be the same for every item that is sold from a single listing. If you let your manufacturer handle the packaging, ask them to place this onto the poly bag or the box. Otherwise, you'll need to handle this yourself and add it to your design!

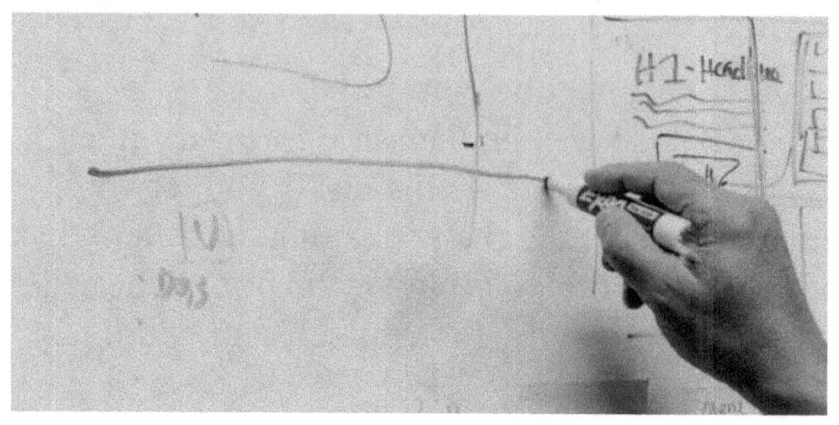

Chapter 5 – Marketing and Selling

Now you know everything you need to know in order to *start* selling through Amazon FBA. But starting selling and being a huge success are two different things.

As I often say: you could be giving away free gold, but without he right *marketing* n one will know and no one will care! You'll still shift zero units!

So how do you go about making sure that people know your business exists? How do you generate buzz and excitement for your product?

The good news is that there is a way to help people find your products through Amazon itself. But if you want to make even more sales, then you can also try driving people to your listing from *external* sources. More sales and reviews from your products built up this way, will also help you to

Use AdSense

If you're a seasoned internet marketer, it's time to experience what it's like to be on the other side of the AdSense equation! You pay just a few cents for clicks, and then you can convert these clicks into potential sales which can earn you huge profits. Learn how to write your advertising in such a way that you only attract people who are likely to part with their cash and you won't face too much wasted marketing, and consider using some of the other pay per click advertising networks too, Facebook for instance. Facebook is especially good as it allows you to target buyers who fit your buyer persona (meaning they're highly targeted by demographic etc.) whereas Google lets you target people that have "intent to buy," meaning that they're interested in buying the product you sell *at that moment* and are likely searching for places to do just that.

By driving enough traffic to your listing this way, you can increase your sales, your reviews, and ultimately your discoverability. Even if the cost of advertising eats into your sales in the short-term then, it can help you to earn significantly more from sales in the long term.

Run a Blog

One of the best and most valuable ways to promote your products through an external channel, is through a blog. Running a blog gives you a direct route to a large number of highly "engaged" viewers. That means they are people who love what you have to say, and who have come to trust your opinion and the information you share. Through a blog (or alternatively a social media account), you can eventually grow to become an influencer. At this point, you have not only a direct route to market, but also a large number of warm leads who are *far* more likely to buy from you.

Consider two scenarios. In one, you are browsing the web, and you see an advert for a product from an unknown brand. It's something that you're vaguely interested in, but not hugely invested in: let's say you're a boxer and it's a pair of boxing gloves.

Now imagine the second scenario: as a boxer, you have been a long-time follower of an amazing boxer and YouTube presenter. They have lots of great ideas and tips and they have a great brand and style that you respond to. *They* then announce that they're selling an amazing pair of boxing gloves, which they hand picked and helped to design for the bet performance, sporting their brand.

Which are you more likely to buy?

Building a loyal audience takes a huge amount of time, effort, and commitment. But in terms of the difference it can make to sales, it is *more* than worth it.

Creating Buzz

Better yet? Use your audience and your route to them (be that a blog, YouTube channel, Instagram account, or email marketing list), and then start creating buzz.

A few ways you can do this include:

With a great trailer or advertisement

With a preorder (which could include a discount – you can use WooCommerce (www.woocommerce.com) or a similar tool to set this up)

With a countdown page

With competitions and giveaways

By asking for advice and ideas

Creating buzz this way is a fantastic method for generating interest and for massively increasing your orders on day one (which translates to a higher position on Amazon and more sales in the years to come). Not only that, but by taking pre-orders you can actually gauge interest in your product, and even fund that initial order!

More Options

Still need more help getting people to find your products? There are nearly limitless options for marketing your products, especially with this kind of business model. Here are some more suggestions:

Influencer marketing/sponsorships
Banner ads
Print media/television advertising
Press releases

Chapter 6 – Photography and Product Descriptions

Hopefully, you've followed the advice in earlier chapters and have chosen an *awesome* product. And hopefully, you're now marketing it well so that a huge amount of people are rushing to place their orders.

But there are still several pieces of the puzzle missing. For example: your store listing!

It's all very well having the best product and a great means of driving people *to* that product, but if the listing doesn't make the product sound great… then you're not going to sell many units!

Here's how to make sure you avoid that mistake.

Description

First, you need to ensure that your product description is on point. So, what makes a great product description?

Firstly, this should be concise and to-the-point. Remember that people are in a rush and *respect their time*. When someone finds your product listing, they don't have time to read through small print to find out what it does or what the key features are. So, get *straight* to the point with a very clear explanation of what your product is, and why it is superior to the competition (that last bit is important!). The worst thing you can do is to open your description with a lot of fluff and sales patter – people will just get bored and leave!

Another tip is to use bullet points. This is an excellent way to get across the key details of your product, as well as to sell your audience on what makes it great.

Remember to use emotive language, and to help paint a picture of the product's physical presence and shape. Try watching a video of Steve Jobs unveiling a new Apple device, you'll find that he would use lots of words designed to evoke elegance, premium build, quality and sleekness. As you can't be physically there to *hold* the product, the aim instead is to help them imagine that they are – and to make it seem amazing.

That emotive language also needs to describe what the product does though. So, think about why people buy products like this, and about what they hope to achieve. Does it make them sexier? More confident? Wealthier? More professional?

Find this "value proposition" and use your sales language to sell the dream. Not sure how to do all that? Then hire a writer who can!

Photography

One of the most important aspects of your store listing is the photograph. This is one of the first things people will see, and it will have a far bigger emotional impact than the product description – at least initially.

This is another crucial reason to order a copy of the product you want to sell! Once you do, here's how to take amazing photographs:

The Tools

First of all you should start out by having the best tools for the job. This means investing in a good high definition camera that is good at capturing light and has plenty of settings. Without investing in a good quality camera your images won't look professional and this will reflect negatively on your products.

As well as having the best cameras it is also worth investing in good lighting, a good camera stand and the best photo editing software so that you can really create the best and most professional looking images.

The Setting

Next you need to think about the elements you want in your image. For some products and purposes the best set up will be to have your item set against a white background with no other elements in shot. More often though it will be useful to include a context for your product so that you can show how it is meant to be used and so that you can create a 'scene' around it.

When doing this you need to think about the associations that you will be creating when you choose these elements. Try to create an image filled with attractive and desirable elements because this will in turn make your product appear more attractive and desirable too.

The Composition

The composition of your image refers to the way that you are going to be setting up all those individual elements and the way that you are going to feature the product in relation to that. Your image should have depth, it should be framed, and it should be designed such that your product be the undeniable focus of the shot.

When creating this image, you should look for lines that will guide the viewers' eyes and think about how these can bring your product into focus. For instance if you were to promote a house, then including a path in the foreground leading to the house in the mid-ground would automatically lead the eye to the main focus of the piece.

The angles you take on your item can also have a big impact on the way it is perceived. For instance if you want to give your product more drama and make it look bigger and more important at the same time, you should try using an 'upshot' that makes it look as the product is towering over the viewer.

Chapter 7 – SEO for Amazon Products

SEO stands 'Search Engine Optimization' and describes the process of optimizing a website or anything else for a given search engine. In other words, if you have a website or blog and you want to maximize the number of people that are visiting, you will likely use SEO techniques in order to get it to rank more highly for various search terms on Google.

This way, if you have a website selling hats in Southampton, you'll now be able to ensure that when someone searches 'buy hats Southampton', your site is one of the ones that comes up first. Of course, it takes a lot of time and effort but this is the basic concept and it can provide excellent ROI seeing as most people use Google to find what they're looking for online.

But Google is not the only search engine. Of course there's Bing, but moreover there are also multiple different search engines built into specific services. The second largest search engine in the world in fact is YouTube!

Another example of a search engine is Amazon (you probably knew this was where I was going with this). Amazon is first and foremost an e-commerce store but with thousands upon thousands of products to sell, it needs a system in place for people to navigate around and find the ones they're looking for. Thus, it has a search engine built in which lets people quickly find the specific items they want.

And as with Google, there are ways that the savvy seller can 'optimize' for that search engine to ensure that their products show up for a large number of search terms. Here we will look at some of those…

Keywords and Keyphrases

When you're using any type of search engine to look for a product, you will tend to do so by typing in a particular word or phrase. If you were using Google to try and information about raising a dog for instance you might type: 'tips for dog owners'. On Amazon meanwhile you might be looking for hats (again) so you might type 'hat' or 'trendy hat' or 'hat for men'.

This is what you call a keyword or a keyphrase and that's what you want your listing to show up for. How do you do that? By ensuring that you have keyphrases embedded into your text – that means adding the words a few times in order to make sure that your text matches what people are searching.

The tricky part though is that you need to a) choose the right keyphrases and keywords to begin with that people are actually look for and b) use the right keyword 'density' in order to ensure you have the right number of phrases for the size of your text. If you 'overdo it' then you can risk your listing looking like it's trying to spam the system and that could lead to penalization. Not only that, but it will make your listing look like spam to potential customers. There's no point getting to the top and then turning people off with your patter!

A common strategy for many business owners is to use their keyword in the product title itself. This can be a great way to quickly get to the top of the SERPs (Search Engine Results Pages), but again you need to avoid letting this harm your branding or your reputation. You can always use a combination:

KiloGlove – Boxing Glove for Martial Arts
Rather than just:
KiloGlove
Or:
Boxing Glove for Martial Arts
Many of the best keyword tools, such as KeywordTool (www.keywordtool.io) actually let

you search for the top ranking search terms on Amazon. This way, you can see precisely what people are looking for, and then customize your products's description to match!

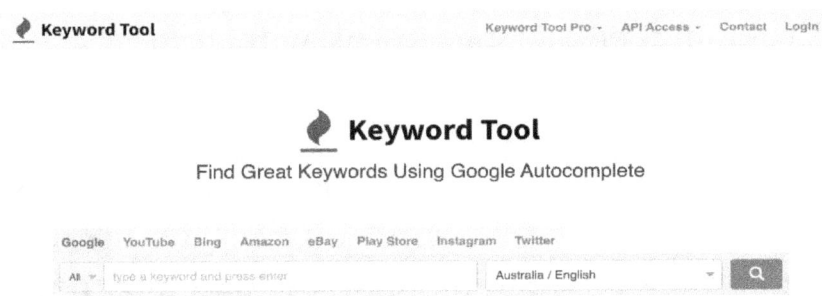

Rating and Reviews for Amazon Products

The rating that your product has is also an important point which can have a big impact on your ranking which is a metric that doesn't apply to other search engines like Google (though it does to YouTube of course!). Make sure that your product is good and that your description is clear – remember that you want to 'under promise' and 'over deliver' if you're trying to get the best reviews.

Another important tip is to respond quickly to negative reviews. If you can give a good explanation and perhaps offer compensation, then reviewers might even improve their score.

Of course, your reviews can also directly influence individual sales for better or for worse. Make sure that a few bad reviews don't make potential buyers turn to your competition. You can improve your average review in a few ways:

Overdeliver by offering something for free or under-promising on delivery times

Reduce the price to ensure amazing value

Listen to feedback and speak with your manufacturers to fix issues

Never ask for reviews!

This is just the tip of the iceberg when it comes to Amazon SEO. Make sure you consider the different ways to rank more highly and incorporate those into your Amazon strategy and you should find you can greatly increase your sales and profits.

Chapter 8 – Alternative Options

One of the best things about Amazon FBA, is that it shows internet entrepreneurs such as marketers, that it is possible to apply their skills and sell something *real* to real customers. Rather than doing SEO for companies that make websites, for companies that sell online courses… you can instead sell a real product direct. *A real business*.

And you don't need a warehouse, a business qualification, or anything else that you don't already have access to/use on a regular basis in your current model.

But now that you've made that realization, the floodgates are open. What other types of business could you build?

Creating Your Own Products

One option is to consider creating your own products and then sending these to customers via FBA. This is a good strategy, but it does involve several new challenges – such as creating your 3D model and creating your bill of materials (BOM).

An easier option? Think of a tweak or a change you can make to a product you're selling, or something that your competition is selling. Not speak with the manufacturer and ask them to consider making the change and letting you sell it exclusively.

It really is that simple! Congratulations: you're now an inventor!

Selling Beyond Amazon

If you're selling a product and you're looking for the next step, then getting it into a Big Box store such as Wal-Mart has got to be one of your main objectives. Not only does this make a lot of sense from a business standpoint, ensuring that your product will be seen by as many people as possible and that it will be available for anyone interested to buy, but it also makes a lot of sense personally. When you see your product on the shelves of a big retailer you will really feel as though you've made it and that's one of the most rewarding parts of being an entrepreneur.

So the question is, how do you even *start* going about getting your product into those stores? It's not as impossible as it may seem, but you *do* need to be logical and methodical in your approach. Read on and get ready to enter the big leagues…

Step 1 - Do Your Research

If you approach retailers without doing any research first you're only going to be wasting everyone's time (primarily your own). For starters you need to know beforehand whether a company is even likely to carry products like yours, and for this you need to research the kinds of things they tend to sell and who their main shoppers are. A good way to find potential outlets is to search for products from your competitors and then see where they are being sold.

Next you should learn everything you can about those stores. Look at their retail guidelines and see if they have a 'product submissions' page on their website (Wal-Mart for instance has step-by-step instructions right on their website!). The more prepared you are, the better chance you will have.

Step 2 - Know Yourself

Likewise you also need to know everything you can about your product and about your business model. When your present your proposal to retailers, you need to be able to show them *why* you're confident it will sell, who your target demographic is and how much it can sell for/how much profit the store will make.

Again the more detail you go into, the more confident stores will be in you and your product. Providing product samples is a good strategy if you can and providing extra materials such as POS displays (point of sale) can help you to win extra brownie points. Press coverage etc. can also help you to win your case.

Step 3 - Find Your Ally

Now you have your pitch/package ready you need to find someone who's willing to listen. Start by contacting the buyer using the details on the website or by calling up and asking to speak to the buyer or representative. If you get snubbed though or don't get any response, you can always try again by looking for contacts you might have within that organisation (LinkedIn is a powerful tool in that regard) or by arranging a meeting with anyone you can. If you can get just one person to listen and to get enthusiastic about your product, then they might help you to get the meeting you need.

Step 4 - Use a Sales Representative

If you're still not having any luck, then another option is to use a sales representative who will handle this part of the process for you. It costs money and you lose some control, but they have experience and contacts which can help them to get you noticed. However you go about it though, don't give up. You can get a thousand rejections but when you get one positive response it will all be worth it!

Chapter 9 – Scaling Your Business

Now that your business is running smoothly and you have your orders coming in fast, you might start thinking about how to take your business further. How do you scale and grow, and become a giant?

Basic Growth

Of course, the most basic way to scale a reseller business is simply to keep reinvesting your money into more inventory and advertising.

Here, you will use the profits from one bulk order and then use these to make a slightly larger order the next time, while also spending a little more on advertising. Each time you sell off your entire inventory, skim off your own "salary," and then take this to invest in more.

While this can work extremely well though, you will eventually need to diversify and create a portfolio of products. VERY few businesses get rich by selling jut one thing!

This is once again where having a brand can become extremely useful.

Branding

So, it's time to move on to your *next* product. But before you do that, you first need to consider building a BRAND.

If you are currently selling a single product to people who don't know anything about your business, then you are not creating any incentive for them to be excited by a potential "second product" from you. On the other hand though, if you can create a brand around your product, then suddenly people will be far more likely to buy from you next time.

You can create a brand by designing a logo and choosing a name for your business. From there, you can then include this on:

Packaging

The products themselves (look for a white-label manufacturer)

Invoicing

More importantly though, you're going to create a website, blog, YouTube channel, Instagram presence.. or all of the above!

This way, you can build an audience, gain trust and engagement, and then use this to create more interest in what you're selling. This is how you turn your products into "must have" items and generate buzz for whatever you do next… before you even know what it is!

With an army of loyal fans, you'll find that your growth comes MUCH quicker and faster.

Other Fulfilment Companies

One thing to consider is that there are other fulfilment companies out there that will provide all the same services as Amazon FBA. Just do a quick search for 'fulfilment service' and you'll find that you have lots of options in your local area. This is a great choice if you want to get around Amazon's issues with selling internationally.

And if you also combine this with a WooCommerce store or another eCommerce store on your own website, then you can use that to sell to your customers directly – reducing the overhead significantly and controlling the experience for your customers more tightly.

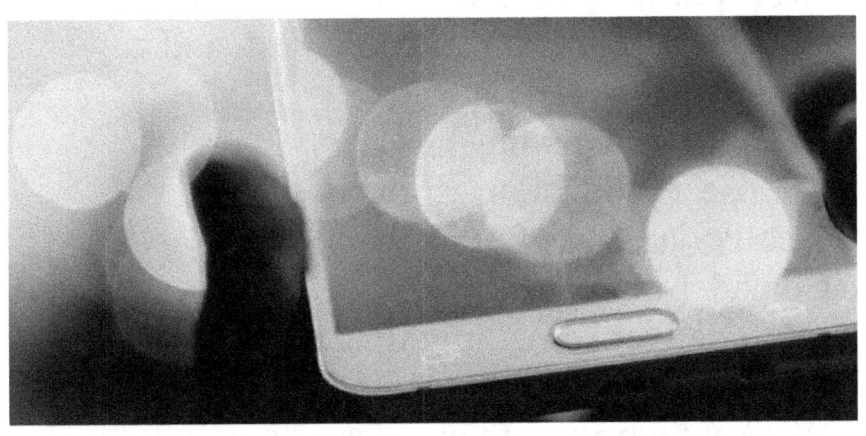

Chapter 10 – Conclusion and Blueprint for Success

Being highly successful on Amazon FBA is simple and it isn't. While this is definitely something that anyone can do, it's also something that requires a fair few steps and can be quite "fiddly."

Hopefully, this book will have walked you through the process, to the point that you feel comfortable diving in and launching your first product on Amazon – all without going near a warehouse or an envelope.

To recap, here are the things you need to consider in order to start selling:

Create an Amazon Account

Choose personal or professional, choose your country

Choose a product category/type

- Research what is selling well on Amazon
- Consider the niche you know best, and any audience you already have
- Create a store listing
- Choose a product on Alibaba
- Ideally one that offers a white-label service
- Consider discussing tweaking the product with them to deliver something unique
- Calculate the Amazon fees, delivery costs, etc.
- Workout a price and make sure you will be making a profit
- Buy a barcode
- Get the wholesaler to send attach the barcode and place your items in packaging. Then they can send the product to your freight forwarder OR:
- OPTIONAL: Involve contract packaging companies to handle the packaging for your individual items
- Get freight forwarding to deliver your products to the country (such as Flexport)
- Prepay for your delivery and get a shipment ID
- Get a carrier to take your products to Amazon (usually UPS)
- Start selling your product
- From here, there are a few things you can do to ensure success:
- Write a great product description
- Use SEO and keywords – do your research
- Get great reviews – overdeliver and respond quickly
- Try lowering the price to drive sales and raise your position in the SERPs

Market using:

AdSense

A blog

You can then consider growing your business by:

Designing your own products

Selling through stores

Branding and selling through your own site

If it all seems a little daunting at first, then one great way to make it less so, is to choose a product on Alibaba that only requires a small initial order. Buy 5 items rather than 10, and then try the business model on a small scale before going all in.

Once you see how well it works – and how much fun it is – then the sky is the limit!

Chapter 11 - Checklist

What is Amazon FBA

Amazon FBA is Fulfilment By Amazon
This means that you will by products, have them shipped to Amazon's warehouses, and let Amazon handle logistics
Benefits
This allows companies to avoid the administrative challenge of packaging and sending
It means customers can buy through a service they know and trust
It ensures a great service for the buyer – they can also use Amazon Prime
It places your products on a huge distribution platform
It means you don't need to rent a warehouse, or store huge amounts of inventory in your home
You don't deal with customer complaints/returns/damaged goods

Choosing Products

Choose a product category/type
Research what is selling well on Amazon
Think about your "buyer persona" who will buy this kind of product?
Consider any audience you already have access to

Think about size and weight

Consider price

Generally, it is easier to start with less expensive products and build up when you have confidence

Think about one-use products versus products that get used a lot/consumables

Consider a longer-term strategy based on this starting point

Choose a product on Alibaba

Ideally one that offers a white-label service – get your own brand on the item

Consider discussing tweaking the product with them to deliver something unique

Calculate the Amazon fees, delivery costs, etc.

Workout a price and make sure you will be making a profit

Look at the minimum orders

The Process

Create an Amazon Account

Personal or Professional?

Amazon India, Amazon UK, or Amazon.com?

Create a store listing

Write a great product description

Use SEO and keywords – do your research using tools like KeywordTool

Use SEO in your product name, along with smart branding

Take amazing photos of your product

Buy a barcode

Get the wholesaler to send attach the barcode and place your items in packaging. Then they can send the product to your freight forwarder OR:

OPTIONAL: Involve contract packaging companies to handle the packaging for your individual items

Get freight forwarding to deliver your products to the country where you will be selling

Prepay for your delivery and get a shipment ID and internal barcode

Get a carrier to take your products to Amazon (usually UPS)

Calculate your pricing

Consider the cost per unit

Look at the prices of the competition

Leave space for deals and offers

Consider the cost of freight forwarding, carriers, Amazon fees

Remember that some customers will want returns/some products will go wrong

Start selling your product

Watch the sales, try experimenting by tweaking the design of your listing etc.

Encourage More Sales

Get great reviews

Overdeliver by providing free gifts or under-promising on delivery times

Include free gifts

Make sure that your product is high quality and offers great value

Try lowering the price to drive sales and raise your position in the SERPs

Market using:

AdSense/Facebook Ads

Ads on Google and Facebook can help you reach the right audience for a low fee. They also help to grow your listing's prominence if they drive sales, resulting in long-term benefits.

A blog
Press releases
Print media
Television advertising
Influencer marketing

Create your own brand: make sure that people know and trust your name and see it as a mark of quality, have them looking forward to your 'next product.'

Include your branding on the product and in packaging
Incentivize future purchases with money off deals
Create buzz for upcoming products with pre-orders, competitions, and countdowns

More Options

Designing your own products
You can design a product from scratch using sites like CADCrowd
Or discuss with your manufacturer adding a few tweaks to existing products
Selling through other distribution platforms
Look for other fulfilment companies
Consider adding an ecommerce store to your OWN website, and then linking that with a fulfilment company
Use this option to expand internationally
Try getting your products into high street retailers and other big stores
Start increasing the number of different products you sell

Chapter 12 - The Most Crucial Resources

Amazon.com
www.amazon.com
This is of course the site where you will be selling your products. For international markets, the other sites are:
www.amazon.in
www.amazon.co.uk

Alibaba
www.alibaba.com
Alibaba.com is a site where you can find a near-endless supply of product wholesalers. These companies will sell you items in bulk at a discount, meaning you can then

UPS
www.ups.com
There are countless carriers you can use in order to get products taken from the freight forwarders to Amazon's warehouses. However, UPS comes Amazon-approved and is a very tried and tested option. They are used to working with Amazon, have a very streamlined and efficient service, and don't charge too much.

Freight Hub
https://freighthub.com

One of several freight companies that can help you get your products into the country ready to get shipped to Amazon's warehouses.

Useful Tools and Sites

AMZSCout FBA Free Calculator
https://amzscout.net/fba-fee-calculator/

This free calculator can be used to calculate the fees that will be associated with any given product from Alibaba. That in turn can help you decide if you will actually make profit!

SnapUPC
https://www.snapupc.com/buy-barcodes/

This is a site where you can buy barcodes. Every single item listed on Amazon will need a unique barcode. If you are selling items on someone *else's* listing (perhaps a book) then you won't need to acquire this. But for every other situation, it is important that you get a barcode from somewhere.

CamelCamelCamel
www.camelcamelcamel.com

CamelCamelCamel is an extremely useful website both for Amazon seller AND for customers. The idea is simple: with CCC, you'll be able to track the price of a product, in order to watch it rise and fall. What may surprise you, is to learn that many product prices are worked out based on machine learning and actually fluctuate slightly even within a *single day*.

Of course, for buyers, this allows you to see when an item is at its cheapest and to receive a notification to react and buy. For those of us selling though, it is a useful option to help us respond to competition and to see what the markets are doing.

Keepa
www.keepa.com

Keepa is CCC's big competition and offers a very similar service. However, what makes it different is that it will also allow you to view product histories. That means you can track how the prices have changed over time, thereby seeing the general rise or fall of those prices and predict market trends.

Google Trends
https://trends.google.com

Google Trends allows you to see how search trends change over time, which in turn can help you to gauge the zeitgeist and see what people are interested in. This is very useful for anticipating emerging fads and trends that you can use to guide your buying decisions. Just be wary of being too driven by what's "in" as whatever is in, is likely to be "out" again very soon – potentially leaving you with a lot of unfulfilled inventory if you mistime it.

Jungle Scout
www.junglescout.com

Jungle Scout is an *extremely* useful tool, that will allow you to do a search of Amazon products and see which ones are selling best. This is very powerful as it allows you to choose products that people are actually buying, thereby nearly guaranteeing your success. Add a tweak, undercut the price, and profit!

WooCommerce
www.woocommerce.com

WooCommerce is an ecommerce store you can easily add to a WordPress site. Why not sell through your own channel too?

Short.CM
www.short.cm

A useful tool for shortening URLs. This makes it much easier for you to share links to your product in emails, blog posts, through social media and more.

Keyword Tool
www.keywordtool.io

Keyword Tool lets you see what people are searching for for SEO purposes. It's not cheap (at all), but it is extremely powerful. Not only that, but it also lets you search what people are looking for on Amazon specifically.

Crowdsourcing Ideation and Design

If you plan on creating your own products for Amazon FBA – which is a brilliant end goal to have in mind – then you might need some help with the design process and providing such materials as the BOM (Bill Of Materials) for your manufacturers. In that case, this list can help you get started.

Idea Bounty
www.ideabounty.com

A great site where you can get people to submit suggestions and ideas for how to create your products. Big brands use this site!

CrowdSpring
www.crowdspring.com

Get everything from your 3D model to your BOM handled by experts and again, only pay for the ideas you like.

CADCrowd
www.cadcrowd.com
Very similar to Crowspring.

Blender
www.blender.org
The best free tool for creating your own 3D models.

Cadsoft Eagle
www.cadsoftusa.com
An example of a CAD program for creating circuit boards.

Useful Reads

How to Successful Market Products on Amazon & Think Like A Buyer
https://www.bigcommerce.com/blog/amazon-marketing-strategy/
A fantastic guide with a lot of great tips that can really help you to sell more.

Hacking Kickstarter: How to Raise $100,000 in 10 Days
http://fourhourworkweek.com/2012/12/18/hacking-kickstarter-how-to-raise-100000-in-10-days-includes-successful-templates-e-mails-etc/
This article from Tim Ferriss shows how to hack Kickstarter and even provides successful email templates and more.

Kickstarter is a great option for those hoping to sell through Amazon FBA, as it can provide the funds to get you that initial big order. Of course, this works best if you plan on selling something new.

How to Write an Effective Landing Page
http://www.businessknowhow.com/internet/landing-page.htm

This post does what it says on the tin and shows you how to create a more successful landing page! This applies to us, because we'll be making a store listing which works in a very similar way.

How to Take Gorgeous Product Photos
https://www.practicalecommerce.com/How-to-Take-Gorgeous-Product-Photos

There are many different facets to a successful Amazon business. Photography is one that often goes overlooked, which can end up really crippling sales. Read this guide and make sure that doesn't happen to you!

How to Master Amazon SEO and Move Your Products Up the Search Rankings in 2019
https://www.bigcommerce.co.uk/blog/amazon-seo-strategy

This post explains how to perform SEO on Amazon, ensuring that your products are easily discoverable for those that want to buy them.

www.ingramcontent.com/pod-product-compliance
Lightning Source LLC
Chambersburg PA
CBHW072033230526
45466CB00020B/1916